STEEL WINGS

STEEL WINGS

Wendy Bardsley

HEADLAND

First published in 1998
by
HEADLAND PUBLICATIONS
38 York Avenue, West Kirby,
Wirral, Merseyside. L48 3JF

Copyright © Wendy Bardsley 1998

British Library Cataloguing in Publication Data.
A full CIP record for this book is available from the British Library.

ISBN: 1 902 096 05 3

All rights reserved. No part of this publication may be reproduced, stored in a retrieval system, or transmitted in any form, or by any means, electronic, mechanical, photocopying, recording or otherwise, without the prior written permission of the publisher.

Requests to publish work from this book must be sent to Headland Publications.

Wendy Bardsley has asserted her right under Section 77 of the Copyright, Designs and Patents Act 1988 to be identified as the author of this book.

HEADLAND acknowledges the financial assistance of North West Arts Board

Printed in Great Britain by
Gee & Son Ltd, Denbigh.

Contents

Sleepers	7		Dream	35
Mrs. Willoughby's Kiss	8		Parallel Paths	36
The Maid's Tale	9		Roots	37
Exodus	10		Restitution	38
Pirate	11		Wiping the Slate	38
Legend in Avalon	11		After the Fruit	39
Old Agenda	12		Footsteps	40
locus standi	13		Contemplation	41
Dark	13		Voyage	42
The Reckoning	14		Moving Place	42
Winter Solstice	15		Male Trepanned Skull	43
Last Words	16		Recitative	44
Young Woman at Twilight	16		Whispers	45
Renaissance	17		Through the Fire	46
Desire	17		Puppet	47
Mrs. Beelzebub Remembers	18		Pebbles	47
Monsoon in Bangladesh	19		Red Mangrove	48
Celebration	20		Werneth Low	49
Sons and Fathers	21		Cheshire	50
House	22		Last Season	51
Till Divorce Us Do Part	23		Inside the Dawn	52
Minus Point	24		Glass Butterfly	53
The Offering	25		Tree	54
Children	25		Moon Lover	55
October Apples	26		Poppies	56
First Place	27		Voices of Time	57
The Curse	28		Eye of Algae	57
The Visit	28		Agatha	58
Reaching	29		Jack O'Lantern	59
Fanfare	30		Sphinx	60
Maya Ceramic Figure	32		Ward Three	60
Ghost Dance	33		Circling	61
The Answer	33		Biography	62
Seraph	34		Elizabeth I	63
Night Visitor	34			

For H. R.

Sleepers

What demons pushed me out too soon,
while you slept in the sanctuary of Time,
until the curfew told them of my dying light.
For spite they sent you then, proud as a bold new bud,
beautiful young god.

We talked of willows and an English spring.
You were a windbreak on a wild shore,
where a torrent raged.
And I knew then why lightning flashed,
and thunder roared.

I burn behind Time's lattice.
How dare I love you now?
The years contract and leave their breath behind.
Sweet mystery,
can Proteus change us into something new;

a whisper through the trees,
a veil of mist, a memory.
This need for you can never end,
this longing will fall
into the maelstrom and cry on, and on.

Mrs. Willoughby's Kiss

(For Buxton Opera House)

A kiss. A kiss. A kiss. This stage
rages on while warm hearts beat.
What then? That cherub there,
on that proscenium arch,
he bangs his tambourine.
He'd have them come again, those names –
He'd raise their skeletons. He would.

The pulse of this place urges on:
love, hate, virtue, pain,
treading the boards.
Once a fire came close, but did not dare.
They say a flame of Edmund Kean
rose in the air.
His bones creaked through the door.

His breath, the morning light,
sings out litanies of love,
bristling on the moor's chest,
whistling through dry stone walls.
This mad play called *Theatre,*
though it were stabbed to death,
would always rise again.

(*Mrs. Willoughby's Kiss* is the title of the play performed at the opening of the Opera House, Monday, 1st June, 1903.)

The Maid's Tale

(After Dietrich Fischer-Dieskau)

How could she have thought
that playing the coquette with Schubert
would have been enough?

Her maid, I held my secret close.
The Countess did not know.
His music raged inside my bones.
I trembled in corridors, yearning.

My skirts were heavy as I climbed the stairs.
I tingled to the sound of his melodies,
those sustained notes;
the sharp edge of his need.

I had to have him now! And now!
So shun me if he must.
He could do what he would –
'*Sie heiβt – die Sehnsucht! Kennt ihr sie?*'

He claimed me daily, his instrument.
The fever of his kiss,
his urgency,
was harmony – not for the ear

but for the blood.
And I must have its swollen flood, its song.
No pastorale. No dream.
This was his fire!

Though somewhere in its ravishment
I felt the tread of death;
a minor key . . .

It was self-destructive of me
to have taken him like that.
No other man can hold me now
without I do not think of him.

Exodus

Self-deceit comes home at last,
trades its dream-eyed essences for flesh.
My spirit seeks a distance. There's the rub.
Its stride has lost its pace
and wanders now through pain's integrity.
My fingers flutter,
caged birds seeking holes to fly through,
to the place where face finds grace
and does not recognise itself.
I'll tear the blood's twist from my cells
and spread my steel wings,
pulse the cavities of space
that make of beauty what it is.
I know the score.
I'll do it now.
I have tried and tried again.
I cannot bite love to the core.

Pirate

Cut-throat rover of the high seas,
you anchor my dreams.
Diamonds bounce
on the sunlit waters of my mind.
I flutter bat-like,
shadow crossing the full moon,
sludge of silence, foolish.

I have walked your plank, bold,
disgust of glitters that were never gold.
Worms have plugged the hold of my conscience.
Now I cruise the long coasts of my mind,
searching frantically,
the sea-stained map
that brought you to my shore.

Legend in Avalon

The ruins of this abbey are thick with rumour.
They buried Arthur here, I think.
Too many centuries past, the ghosts prevaricate,
forget their messages.
Our week has run its course.
We have plucked the sacred apples from the magic tree,
unfolded the sky and stored our secrets
in its curvilinear heart.
Merlin stands by Glastonbury Tor
and talks with Arthur's ghost; the one I parched who fled.
My Lancelot, we rode the hurricane,
steadied the crazed flame of our limbs with love.
Our tone poem sings in earth.
We are defined in burnished stone,
in leaf points reaching, bones of beasts.
The universe is caught in this, the stuff of stars.
I shall remember the stillness of these shadows,
the way your lips meet mine, for the last time,
in the cold chill of this passing breeze.

Old Agenda

He masked his demons, spun them,
heard them laugh,
her voice whispering down corridors,
blushing windows.
Once he saw her face pressed to the glass.

He thought he'd pulled her out
by every root
from the racked quick of his heart;
a crisis of rotting roses, soft hair,
peaches bruised.

This second love is hollow,
whistles through the black holes of its skull.
He locks the doors and windows.
On the still edge of his thought, *she* waits.

locus standi

She said it was not her best love.
She offered her mouth, her body, her embrace.
After that, she could not say.

In exchange, he was silent,
preparing vegetables, chopped precisely,
neat and careful shapes,
the sad leaves of lettuces cast aside,
only the crisp stark hearts left.

He brought her fruit –
oranges, apples, cherries –
washed and pressed the white cloth,
dazzled her with it,
lit candles that lent essences and winked.

He did not fit the blueprint of her thinking.
But she offered her mouth, her body, her embrace.
After that, she could not say.

Dark

Darkness has stolen all the light,
and time has swallowed all her days.
Innocence has closed the door.
Tinder of anger, loss and pain . . .
Love's ghosts are chattering again
with the pitiless voice of emptiness.
Bring me Adonis flowers,
and let them flame
in the hole that used to be my heart.

The Reckoning

This is the foulest place.
The red desire gnawed white,
and battered. Done to death.
The heavy whole that will not part,
its essence spent
on the ice cold edge of fire.
It does not stir.
It is a snakebite, belladonna, hemlock,
young as spring without its daring,
shutting itself away;
a rook that only knows the night,
drunk with sorrow, its dark shroud eternal,
smothering the dawn.
In this valley we beg for time,
and are abandoned here.
The years fall in between.

Winter Solstice

I pause,
like the sun at the solstice,
full moon rising,
dreaming the diamond
beamed on too intense that turned to dust.

I have cut off my sensitivities.
They writhe like snakes.
Pegasus has tried for birth
from the Medusa's blood –
Hooves and wings and things.

Where would he take me?
Only with you
does Time seem worth the breath.
Our love falls like spring blossom,
pink mouths caught in a collector's net,
silent with sadness.

Your memory forces through my blood.
All day you course my veins.
I am talking to empty paving stones,
walking alone.

Last Words

Enough. I curse you virtue!

You are burnt out like an autumn leaf,
with nothing left of thankfulness.
You twist in the mulch of other element.
Your name is lost.

What thread connects to what you started at.
What source. What end.
You are gathered in the magician's fist:
white cloth that bursts into a dove and flies.

Young Woman at Twilight

I think it's finished.
The paint still wets my tongue.
My back's against the wall, I know,
but I shall break through this still life tonight,
crawl out dizzy-eyed, like a grey hernia, from its belly.

The space is cold.
My nerves are racked from the storm of his brush.
He's steered right off the track, forgot the tender turn.
The plot's gone wrong, colludes with lies.
This picture slurps, gobbles itself quick.

Renaissance

Dissect it then, the fine art of our love.
Piece by piece, examine it.
Lay it out, line by line, angle on angle.
Separate and spend its mystery.

My muscles ache
with the pull of love's wheel
turning on its own teeth,
finding its way like beauty in darkness.

What can I retrieve. What will you spare.
I measure the tool of your eye.
Demons are human in Renaissance hell, you know.
You do.

I wait.
The theme recedes to symbol, myth.
I hold my breath and listen to my clay's core,
as you try my stone another time.

Desire

Remembering you in the still hot night,
words tumble down the slope of sense
like beads lost from their thread.
And longing grows, like a pause
in which a million years are spent.

The ghost inside my mirror knows
that is has fetched its own.
It mined through hell to get to you.
Come, be with me in the wild valley.
Swirl inside my hurricane.

This year's fruit will not be taken by the worm.

Mrs. Beelzebub Remembers

When I got home that day,
he was sitting in his study reading.
He read lots of theology
and stories about supernatural phenomena.
Occasionally I'd see him reading mathematics,
though I never knew what he did with it.

I feared for the universe.
He went off for weeks, whole months sometimes.
God knows where. Now and again, he said,
there'd been an intersection in the road
and he'd lost his way.
Though he always came back.

He knew he was beautiful.
I'd watch him stand against the dark sky,
rocking triumphant.
He understood the human mind so well,
knocked its skittles down in one go
with his home-grown majesty.

Much surer stuff than the other,
needing all that packaging and labelling
to the right address.
No-one ever re-directed all that love
if it went astray.
It stayed in corners. Grew mouldy. Forgotten.

From time to time he'd bring it home and smile.
It was like a baby.
He'd like to have given it some of what he'd got.
Though if he did,
he knew he'd get it back again,
and bite for bite, where would he be then?

He'd thought about it though, a lot.

It was an enigma.
Lately he'd grown bald with worry,
having lost his influence.
What he'd done, seemed to have its own momentum.

Love, was the curse, he said.
It could burn its own heart out
with the fury of its flame.
He knew all about that.

Monsoon in Bangladesh

After the trees were torn away, the land gave in
and lost itself in that ferocious rain.
We squatted in our huts, held fast to earth.
Our mothers thrust their arms out in the space
where the deluge burst the roof: *Forgive us* . . .

It was wanton that year, eager as loosed rock,
prised apart and freed.

My father held my brother shoulder high
sheathed in water, but they did not make the boat.
I often hear him tell it. Like absolution now.
How he found the flowered shirt,
fluttering in the sacred tree, in the dry season.

Celebration

My baffled art has found its place in you;
the light's surprise.

I am all wings, all elegance,
a white swan on a lake,
heavy with pride.

I lift you to my breast. Your song swells
from the well where lightning rests,
sings through the labyrinth of my days.

My child –
Where were you then? And then?
Your tender spark has fired my heart.

Sons and Fathers

(For D. H. Lawrence)

So in the end he lied,
about the house.
We read between the lines
that he put passion first, more truth in that.
He won her with his eyes, his dance.

And did she want the truth at last.
Or would she rather sail with him,
round the edge of the story:
a gathering storm that would not break.

Niceties? He might have given her those.
He'd stumbled on the rose,
the shock of the hawthorn blossom,
wet on his way back from the pit.
The fragrance brought her burning in his veins.

He understood the son's burden.
The lad had documented that all right.
But lover? No.
He didn't know the half of it.

Art's no grit to a miner.
The blood, the spit, is where he's at,
filling the gaps of the dry stone walls
where the truth's lies whistle through.
Where the truth's lies whistle through.

Where the truth's lies

whistle

through.

House

You are mute and desolate.
The children's things
are beginning to smell of age.
Their little books of fairy tales
live only through the book mite now.
The doors groan disenchanted
creaking their old arthritic joints.

What drama played in here.
What Christmas parties urged it on.
I can still hear wrapping paper
crackling round the Christmas gifts.
The lights too, on the tree told lies.
Like you and me.

Who is this child I see? My son?
A grown man now.
I dreamt of him last night.
Time moves on indifferently,
sometimes leaves us
lost on barren shores
with only land and sky. And land and sky.

Till Divorce Us Do Part

(People seem to view divorce as an alternative to talking to each other) Options: January 1995

They did not talk.
Instead they danced on circumstance,
its crevices perilous;
sailed a gambler's sea,
their frail sails bursting.

Only the cuticle of the night
could seal their suffering from its pain.
It surfaced daily with the dawn
and drowned the day,
its truth lost in the plumage of the clouds.

If only words had been allowed to break that capsule,
clinging like a sick prayer,
essences apart,
preserved from the rot of compromise.
Even intuition dared not raise its eyes.

They did not talk.
They danced instead on circumstance,
its cold edge brutal with decision.
Precision tools, they found their way to another pit,
the tongue and grooving of their hearts
secure, inseparable, intact.

Minus Point

The pack is heavy.
Here the last plus meets its minus.
Giving forfeits what it was,
at the minus point along the line.

She's done the maths.
She knows the knot she can't untie.
The children stare.
Their eyes roll, white with loss.

The minus road.
Who knows her pain? Who lends a plus?
She walks alone.
No-one comes home to this.

The Offering

Your tiny body stirs.
Your frail amethyst wings
are like an evening summer sky.
I wonder at your eyes –
those silver lashes
all that yellow hair,
like dancing twists of spluttering gold.
Who would leave so rare a child
beneath the lilac tree.
Your wings are cold.
What shall I do.
Ought I to take you, make you mine.
But who will understand.
And will they fear your pale amethyst wings,
the silver cilia that close your eyes.
Those eyes –
What do they see.
What have they seen.
What shall I feed you –
seed from sea moss, moonwort,
marigold and wintergreen.
What shall I teach you baby Queen.
Where do you come from.
You will need me if they laugh
at silver lashes, water coloured wings,
and things like that.

Children

Because they feel the warmth still of the light
and the taste of holiness still lingers on their tongue,
they bear the worst the best. They leap the stars.
They are the ghosts who wait for us
along the road when we are slow, and do not know the way.

October Apples

Only I know the thin scrape of her elbow
beneath my skin,
the nervous flicker of her fingers.
She is here now,
by me in this cot.
I do not even know
the colour of her eyes;
they are tight shut in a vow of silence,
snug in the hold of her death.
The red bell of her heart is stopped,
the little rivers of her veins have stayed their flow.

You have brought the apples in, you say.
The worms are soundless; teeth that gnaw
inside the great dumb mouth of fate.
I have pushed her out cold dead.
An odd gift for the sun.
Tonight you will come
and hold her,
while we cry.

First Place

And so it is over.

The bowl I brought is filled with vomit,
alive with froth. The peace of death
has claimed his face.

The sun runs in – a dazzle of fast fingers,
takes him quickly,
leaving the cold damp flesh with me.

I close his lids.
Where is the grace? What does it mean
when breath has clenched its fist
and punched life from the space?

This sudden stop,
as if some hammer blow had owned the right,
has pulled the shutters tight for him on all seasons.

His fingers cannot span a millisecond now.
The may fly's wings, its fleeting dance,
has better chance.

Where is the sound we called his voice?

He made us laugh.

His skin is smooth,
as if anointed with a sacred oil.
Something has taken what he was.
It haunts the furniture, the pictures, shadows . . .

But it is this rush of feeling owns it. *Here.*

The Curse

This room was always different from the rest.
The sadness of the house resides in here.
No flowers thrive.
The fireplace wears an air of emptiness.

Devoid of love, it reaches for a track to tread,
a place to go. It knows no glow.
Who gave this room the house's doom?
It would not heal, although I tried and tried.

The Visit

How long since last I came?

The years cram fast
inside the hollow of the night.
I am a child again,
my feet on smooth sand;
the inside of the sea's mouth,
my footprints small,
reaching from their nervous tread.
I gather them in, like Oceanus might.
Poor echo! falling on exhausted stone.
Oceanus, once, I know you brought me home,
carried me on the waves, anemones in your hair,
and four sea-urchins on your back,
clutching embryos of sun and stars.

The gulls torment their own reflections.
Their screeches fly to the little house
high on the cliff
where the golden rod taps at the window.
I recall my brother's birth,
new bones ringing new melodies,
the small blot of his face, his quiet breath,
emerging into this new womb.

Reaching

This is your body.
Take ownership. This is your flesh.
You feed daily on thunder and lightning.
It cracks and splits the living tips of your leaves,
confounds their direction.
What is this memory of place?
Your skin smarts with the earth of time's past,
knows the thin veins reaching through darkness,
eyeless as toadstools,
shy as bats twitching in the night air.

Now you beg identity,
flap, featherless,
naked of being,
cold, in a bold contemptuous element.
Your eyes shift to the tops of mountains,
blinking, swallowing their peaks.
Your thoughts ring with the water's memory,
hurrying inside its own space,
back into the sun's heat.

Fanfare

I

It is like a kind of hieroglyphics.
My body is folded in the clay,
like the black curl of a storm cloud.

Give me lightning!
Jolt my heart and start me up.
My small ship stirs
and colours
from the inside of the spectrum try their way.

Hear them in the loud O of the wind!
the raw bite as it passes the face,
the itch it leaves,
the cold twitch in the cells.
I am bone and flesh.
I lift out from the mud and find my shore.

II

This is *kinesis*.
I am moving in the cold promise of mathematics.
You can count me in the noughts and ones of light.
My flesh is bitter. Better spit the pith.

I am the slippery fin of a flying fish.
My rudder of desire is fierce against the ocean's drag.
Let me walk in the honey groves
where the shadows press on the walls of light
and draw no dark.

I am a blaze, a vertigo, a supernova. How long can I flare?
Give me the lair of another's skin.
Peel it. Let me in. I'll spit the pith.

III

It is a brittle land.
I watch my tread.
My pupils burn.
A little at a time I am examining my thoughts.
The bond between myself
and the tap root of my tree has gone.
I am astonished how easily
I have parted from water – my element.
I cup it in my hand and drink.

Already I am losing the secret of the compass,
all is concentrated in the mass behind my eyes.
My queen cell screeches far away. I taste the earth.

My senses are lined with the hair of wolves.
My anatomy is fine-tuned to the sound of being.
I am in a system now of laws, of definitions.
A catalyst, a theory to an act, creation's eye.

Our way is plotted.
We are in an interplay of breath and bone.
– Your line is joining mine. Hold on.
– *Hold on.*

Maya Ceramic Figure

From Campeche, Mexico (IIins)

If you sit squat, facing her, it might happen –
the soft pat of her feet,
the click of her fingers in the dance.

Her torso is smooth as sun.
Steady leaves of fingers have passed through
centuries across her limbs. She is saturated with love.

What tool has sparked those eyes?
The dome of her body is vast with antiquity,
stretching a straight line eye to eye with me.

It is her Golden Age, wet with the echoes of water,
dry with silent time.
She is stopped as a surprised arachnid, her dance stayed,
a Coppelia in her maker's mind –
he might have had her *this*, or *this* . . .

She started when the wet heat bundled into stone,
clinging like the bony weight of bats, an each to each.

We are unable to decipher her pictographs.
Her secrets are safe.
But if I listen hard, she tells me *he* is here,
coursing through her fiery heart,
lacing the necks of hills with mountains,
holding the writhing trees against the wind.
Her left arm reaches out for him in a sigh of sand.

Ghost Dance

Old river of dreams,
your great length stretches this stratum
where I cram inside the niche of space.
You are the quake of the sun,
ears of sound beyond ringing.
I rise with you, lark-like, acquiesce,
decorate myself with the plumage of your colour.

Water-borne being,
shell against its own ear,
curious living tissue of my mind,
I do not ask you here.
You stay, close, skin of stone.
Eyes, ears, tuned into the mind's octave,
waiting, till the maestro calls the dance.

The Answer

It spins
with the rut and cut of a sycamore seed,
twists and turns;
a secret,
eager for openness,
stumbling from its chains
to claim its place,
tearing the fruit from the sweet bough
of the threads of thought,
cavorting clown-like,
flitting, quick and slick as a butterfly
landing in the curved arch of a waiting moon.

Seraph

A burst of flaming wings.
A gust of pale pink nacreous skin.
The quick snarl of a hurricane.
The soft eye of a dove.
The raw and bitter screech of love.
Its hands translucent bones of stone.
A sudden grace.
The Seraph, flaming, shuddering in,
then gone.

Night Visitor

This night has lost the note
that finds the song for wrong.
Its dark form crumbles
in uncharted depths
where love's light lends no beam.

Even the moon has scared itself away,
peers through the hole of day
searching for the heart that glows.
It has escaped the snare of ash.
What now?

Somewhere a light kindles,
bursts like a supernova
from the surface of emptiness,
a recurring stanza,
eager to repair this injury, again.

Dream

One day I woke,
and I was different from before.
And all the people I had ever been
came walking by my door.

These were my ghosts.
But what appalled me most
was having lost their love.

I did not give enough of time
to this long line of yesterdays,
their sufferings on my account,
the special offerings they made.

They did not stop,
although I called and called,
and tried to say goodbye.

Parallel Paths

Someone walks beside me.
Which of us puts first foot forward.
Who has choice.
Something digs for its own talisman.
Its acclamations burst my ears.
It reaches, grasps the purple sinews
of my heart and rides.

Pedlars of terrifying wares
put their stern inside my sea,
their prow on my land.
I cannot reach the bird in me.
I am two elements.
wracked with conspiracy.
Each denies its true inheritance.

Until the spear of truth lances the wound,
sharing its secret alphabet,
repairing the alchemy of despair.
I'll manage this. It comes now,
gentle as a kiss.

Roots

First I traced you with a green crayon,
Old, old, clod of earth; *my country.*

I learned the names of your oceans
and mountains by heart,

finding them
with the end of my finger.

Invasions thudded in, like thunderbolts,
like comets, like hurricanes,

warriors stripping the sea,
stealing the land,

decorating its history
with their own ornament,

placing their feet
in the breaches of its walls,

weaving the fabric of its thought
with their own art,

my mirrors recalling their faces,
their passions stirring in my heart and voice,

my eyes darting to the stars
in one great leap.

Restitution

What is it saves us in the end.
What ghost gives wing.
When as we flounder in the pit –
suddenly, we're out of it.

Wiping the Slate

Silence breaks the sound,
reveals the hole where faith was lost.
The peace escapes,
a raging flame to blind the eyes.
And the torn off limbs of love
search for the souvenirs of what they were
in the hanging boughs of cloud.
I peel the skin from the sun's face,
shift my glance from the mirror
to the heedless willow's dance.
Dreams are all it answers to.
Inspiration stalks my track and penetrates.
The arms of fate reach,
find their hold and draw me back.
I cool now with the moon.
Your pores breathe with my breath.

After the Fruit

A mysterious sickness surrounds them.
Their eyes and ears are stopped with thought.
The rotting stars totter.
Darkness stares dumbfounded,
swallows itself to the place where all things end,
where lies stutter and shadows pretend
at sunlight and healing hands.

Ashes of death blow careless here.
The scent of fruit distorts
what might mistake itself for truth,
pulverised beneath the fast feet of the future,
while today's corpse rises, self-styled, enigmatic,
treading the gangplank once again,
from nowhere to nothing.

Footsteps

You become used
to the way the earth bends its ear
to the weight of a body,
the sky's embrace of sound.
The sun would shoot the wind
to stillness if it could,
wrap itself, a convolvulus
around its heart to steal this echo;
Time defined like flowers
pressed inside a book.

Clumps of possibility,
hang like cobwebs, relics of habit,
footsteps never taken, footsteps lost,
in shadow, on the wrong track,
in a wounded future/past,
howling through winters' nights,
raining on windows,
lashing against the bottled shores of mind.

Contemplation

Some beast hides in this wound.
Each day its growl is muffled.

A hawk grinds at the bones of speech,
preparing the dust.

Devastation and decay hurry,
sure footed, bawling, loud as thunder.

And a flower grows somewhere,
unrecognised, unclaimed.

Push. Here's the road. I've found it now.
The little sparks I left are here,

smouldering in the gutter.
I blow my life's breath through their embers.

We are packed, like snowdrift,
backs against the wall.

I recall the sun once, shuddering with the water
into thought,

stirring my blood all night,
into its lonely light.

Voyage

Somewhere inside me, there is a lore, a myth,
searching anchorage for delivery,
to wake and bloom and start its story once again.
It is behind glass, engraving itself daily,
like frost, its breath unique, its source book secret,
winter boughs against December skies,
fearing for the loss of spring.
I pale traveller, brief gift to the mind,
stretch for the right note in the symphony,
the colour scheme, the pulse, the heart.
What happens in its moment happens then,
Time's essence flavours in its hour.
It has no second thought.
Frail as battered cobwebs grasping the past,
the future is fagged and feverish,
while the tide's cannibal eagerness
takes its sharp nails to the surface of the day,
eager for tomorrow's blood.

Moving Place

It hurts like a jagged edge,
cursing the line it stalked,
steel on steel.

Perception grows,
testing its realm like elastic,
its intention.
I feel the wind's rush, like a lover's passion,

potent, rich,
bending the trees to a victor's arch,
I must go through.

Male Trepanned Skull

Was it your finest demon they set free?
And did they laugh,
and take it for their own?

Give me incantations, the mystic rituals
of earth, air, fire, water –
the magic of the aerial regions,
the variable stars!
Like the muscles
on the inside of the eye,
they grasp the part that sounds the tune.

Slow wanderer through time, exist.
Snatch my energies and grow my heart.
Bright as a cat's eye in the night,
backed by a thousand thousand mirrors,
I *will* see you.
Stretch the ether, feel your trail.
I am here.

Our divided beam folds back.
Your thought vibrates the air,
until I hear it crack –
Remember me, you say. *Today,
remember me.*

Recitative

Out of rubble and gravel, we grew,
caught each other's glances fast;
an eagerness of blood.

All day and all night long
we fingered the moon,
searching for an instrument
on which to play,
the sticky trembling sun
glaring blatant.

We would have called you,
built a site
on which we might have solved.
We would.

Just for a second –
or was it less?
our hearts began.
And we could smell the gentle scent
of evening rain
stirring our sediment.

It did not take us long to die.
We tried to stay.

Whispers

This is where the long exhausted distance ends.
I've walked a straight line, telescopal,
no more room to make the red ring blue,
or bank the coin that might have saved.

I have passed your tree time and time again.
It is without fragrance.
Freedom's blossom hangs
in the balance of your boughs,
whitefaced dead.

I uncurl, a new fern, green and lithe.
There is no sky.
Only a chamber revolving; source of my force,
slippery as a skid.
I am bruised to tears.

I did not find my way to this.
It gathered me into its element,
the great ache of its pull.
Its whispers return daily,
round the sides of this dome.

Through the Fire

Tell me, grey woman, by my side,
dredge your memory and bring the word
from the black hole of your carrion world.
I am a crow, a fox, a demon perhaps,
creeping in the dead of night,
out to kill.

I'll crack the world's egg,
drag its secrets from the shell,
belt them till they yell at last,
and tell me what it is
that glides up by my nest,
and steals my place.

Tell me what the message is in the swish of grass,
the frost that blasts its pattern on the rock,
swallowed fast in a yawn of sun.
Dust of existence, dark translucence,
shoal of blind fish, stalk in wind,
come tell me now!

Did you know the sun before,
the scaly bark of sycamore,
this fit of rain?
You are voluptuous with knowledge.
Stop, eat from your harvest.
Stay now. Do not grieve.

Breathe. Forget.
The mourn will always be imperfect.
It must lick its wounds for ever,
wrap its miseries in a cloak of mist, their colours secret,
muttering low in shrivelled dried out leaves,
the drip of wet berries.

This groan aches and aches because its hour has gone.

Puppet

The curtain rises on your eyes.
And someone else invokes the pattern
for your thought and dance,
takes us with you.
We are true to your tears,
manage your combat precisely.
Your head nods. Moon rider.
You play your part, Masterclass,
empty as cowardice.
Your limbs twist absurd,
like sea, dragged wearily.
Immortal masterpiece,
I know your mind and gesture.
I know who you are.

Pebbles

And shall I take a simple shape at last,
like these pale sisters, silent, still,
regardless of the bluster of my sea, my hurricane.
Poised jewels, beautiful and smooth and cool.
Who can break through to their mystery
and find the passion breathing
in the wild woods of their meek design.
They are the fury and the rage of the beginning,
blazing at the back of Time.
I am a tendril, naked with desire, searching a hold,
invoking *joie de vivre*
from the thin crack of the light.
A guest today,
tomorrow sea-spray on a strange uncharted shore,
or something more I do not know of yet,
although I think I knew of it before.

Red Mangrove

(In the salt or brackish waters of tropical and sub-tropical sea-shores, the red mangrove shows an ability not only to survive and colonise an environment impossible for most other trees, but even to create land.)

I had always feared loneliness;
the fierce strike I must make in the land;
my own mark. I pecked like a bird.
Blight tormented me, like a sharp-nosed shark,
muscling for blood.

I gathered my clans –
ghost warriors of imagination,
gave them the clack and clatter of my tattered thought,
learned the art of the snake's trick on the rock –
dagger of light that hitches its own pitch, grits its teeth.

I am the dark throat tangle of this brackish water.
Before I left my mother tree, I stole a ripeness,
grasped maturity, Time's shutters down,
and struggled like an ancient myth for life.
Seedlings do not grow a root like this.
It was a demon's kiss.

Precocious, I took the mud and showed it serious business,
grew my own brothers and sisters incestuously,
dizzied the earth's head so it could not see.

I have anchored the water graciously,
give succour to its banished and unloved; its flotsam and jetsam.
I embrace them, call them as a mother calls her own at night.
They grow my land. My kingdom.
I have turned the planet inside out.
I watch you come and go. I hear you talk,
about the healing mysteries of my bark.

Werneth Low

My star glows in this place,
ringed in the spin of Cheshire, Derbyshire and Lancashire.

This is the haunt of violets, harebells, celandine,
the fox, the stoat, the weasel,
hawthorn, willow, birch and pine.

I would tear this poem out by its heart and give it name . . .

This is the haunt of violets, harebells, celandine,
the fox, the stoat, the weasel,
hawthorn, willow, birch and pine.

The lake of thought awakes and blinks – a slow surrender.

This is the haunt of violets, harebells, celandine,
the fox, the stoat, the weasel,
hawthorn, willow, birch and pine.

The words won't come.

Close to the bone this poem stays.
Confined in passion it can say no more.

Cheshire

The word is the glossolalia of the wind as it whets the land:
    glissando, pianissimo . . .
It is the exhale of the sleek dance of this northern plane:
        one-step, two-step, heel-toe cavalcade of light –

No hills impede its progress here.
It can place the flat of its palm on this terrain,
translate its excess to a whisper round the shutters of my house,
through the over-flow of the bath-tub
where I sit and soap my limbs, remembering my mother.

        Outside trees sing: *Cheshire* . . .
        Clouds and grasses nod.
        Snowflakes sing it in the winter.
        Bluebells sing it in the spring.

Her memory is defined by things like this,
the free-wheel of ideas, flowers, bubbles in a bath,
washing billowing on a line, the crumble of white Cheshire Cheese
in the steady fingers of her hands.

Last Season

Dark factotum of yesterday,
the year dies on your breastbone.
O Solomon! You dare compete with this?
Who listens here?
The angels sleep, long distance flown,
the rings have fallen from their fingers.

You have pulled the planets through with you,
cast hues on stained glass windows,
on faces raised in prayer,
have told us little tales of devils and of gods
in love's likenesses.

The first tread of your ancestry was bold,
with nowhere else to be,
now the leaf's journey delivers your chronicles,
while the sky's bones stir to hands,
gathering you to other element.

Inside the Dawn

An orange sun rises,
riddles its nest of golden fruit.
Its red heart glows.
Snake come back,
it rattles its blood,
wrestling in perception's net.

And love waits by the golden bait,
for the long note,
lingering beyond the sound;
the charmer's knack.

Its torso twists,
vessel that turns its inside out,
without a crack,
and seeds
to spine, to eye, to mouth, to scream,
retreats to dream.

Solution rides on suffering's back,
dull grave sickened of its own bone,
spring naive of wintering,
wrestling the key from dust and ash,
again.

Glass Butterfly

Some days it seems a desert comes in,
roaming my mind,
a dim mystery of ripples, searching for shadows.
It is like the trill of a bird,
the laughter of a blazing summer.
If I hold my hand before my face,
I see the loneliness of fingers,
like stems of flowers in jars,
in water, choking in its own tears,
rooted by its own weight.

You bring your glistening heart to share my space.
I find my cobweb tracery; a network of desire,
wind-rippled veils of golden dune,
wafting memory, ringing with the songs of sand,
dizzying with the fragrance of white daisies,
yellow eriophyllum, purple nama,
springing from the dust, like glorious brooches
pinned to the breast of an old, old sun.

(White daisies, yellow eriophyllum and purple nama are desert flowers visited by butterflies.)

Tree

The sea will never freeze in me.
Tonight, against this blood-red and magenta sky,
I scratch and lash,
shoot my fangs at the air, like a viper.

Always, somewhere,
I can hear my dark neighbour,
lost in shadow, a multi-headed fiend,
trying to assert itself,
begging for bread.

Each spring I wear my ring, new;
my marriage to the firmament.
It is the motion of clocks,
coming through the hole of darkness,
memory of what it was to reach for warmth
and know the light was near.

For I must feel,
as trumpeter with tongue and lip,
my leaves' tips reaching.
I make exchange with wind and stone,
the rustle of something in your bones;
the earth's dream, seen from my mind's eye.

Moon Lover

Demon tormentor,
Master of seduction,
you strike hard.

I am a fitful jolt
in this convulsing crowd.
Your eye is peeled.

Boastful of glitz
you are tricked out,
jewelled and feathered,
ballast for that chaotic galaxy of dust.

Sweetheart,
I am prey to your moods.
Your vampire bouts bewitch.
All night you stare.

Illustrious adventurer,
I pulsate like a revelling star.
nerves threadbare.

How my head swims
with your greedy aphrodisiac charm!
I am inert.

Like a season without choice
you pummel me to shape,
fasten yourself again,
inside my skin.

Poppies

Wet light April night,
You are bright with poppies,
dancing in the moon's circle;
eyes all eyes.
Their red skins drip.

Close as thistle or nettle
they sting the wind.
Memory does it.
It is made of blood:
the red butterfly
that drains the petal's veins.

Don't look.
Its essence stains my tongue.
Its black eye climbs
from something crouched in me.
Listen.
You can hear its breath.

Voices of Time

This season is blind with indifference; the dream
that steals the heart and leaves the life bereft.
Its long exhale of breath is done,
like hope that first intoxicates and then forgets.

The leaf's tongue is soundless,
its only thought the first bite of the light,
while the earth's throat moistens for another song.

The pregnant gods are succulent
with hell's attempt to find content.
And the music starts, a heavy conscience, fear on fear,
growing a membrane, close, like wind on skin.

Its white bones clutch, again.

Eye of Algae

It stirs,
root hair of blood,
moulding the sieve that grasps the light.
Silence has taught it precision, pattern perfect.

Precursor of glory, kith and kin,
borne on the wind, to stalk, to leaf,
to bone, to flesh, each inch shifting in its own shaft,
let me honour you with prayer, primeval preparer.

Time's long sunbeam has unravelled you
from its ripened core. The stone's surprise.
A flood of light. A spectral glow.
The long low shriek from the grey mist of our cells.

Agatha

I am stitched into the fabric of superstition.
Children peer in through my windows.
I give them the blood-smile of a bat,
flutter and dance moth-like on the glass.
They love my mischief.

Once, they brought me roses.
Fools! You cannot break the rules.
I gathered like smoke, provoked their peace,
turned their fingers black
and speared their thought with lies.

They have watched me slide the rainbow on my back,
right across the meadow.
I stir my anger, chant it up
and bottle it for spite,
my heart's bud wrapped for better time.

They brought me cups of red wine,
ridden with impotence,
spells of glow worms, writhing,
thorns from the hawthorn hedge,
conspiring in my throat.

I threw it to the rats,
roaming the corridors of their fate
and fed the silence of their destinies.

I dress myself in fresh lilies,
the red and gold of autumn leaves.
I dance on cobwebs, wet with dew,
span the sunbeams with my fingers.
Sometimes, you will see me,
in the mirror,
staring from your eyes.

Jack O'Lantern

I can hardly believe it.
It is over a week. Nothing.
The air is flavourless.
I sink in its sloth.
There is not even the light of a candle.

Grace and Luck chant facts like lunatics.
They are without blood, without a heaven,
quarrelling in the night,
breaking my sleep with their futile discussion.

The sound of the real song fades . . .
I have tried to find it in the trees,
swum the rivers and the seas right through,
borrowed Ariel's wings to search the mountain tops.

The soil deva shifts beneath me,
slow, blind as a worm.
I am weary of this wretched space.
Draw me! Breathe me in!

I am heavy with yield,
dance like a genie round an empty lamp,
the number of your last count,
repeating itself, over and over,
a nebulous star,
its wares laid out in darkness.
I deal in barter.
Give me light!

Sphinx

You stand in that corrosive air,
rooted in sand,
a white cave in the sky,
a hump on the sun's back.

Fabulist!
You teller of a million tales,
you go full circle now,
from dust to dust.

The sky,
monotonous with Time,
your plucking post,
rings with the steady chime of stones.

Ward Three

It would have been better
had I been a bird
and flown off.

As it is
I find myself clamped to earth
the corner stone of what I am, crumbling.
The portraits on the walls are dim,
the furnace of my being cold.

Shavings of steel shoot the air.
Their glitter dazzles.
If I reach for you, and you,
I feel their anger,
the chatter of their energy,
at the back of my teeth.

Circling

I

I peel the layers off my skin, and grow again.
Thoughts clatter.
Where do they go? Will they come back?
I am left with the marriage of my history,
like the rings of a tree,
inside the circle of what I am, and what I was.
What shall I be?

Listen. Are those footsteps mine?
Their sound is cut off by the sharpened edge of time.

Silence now.
I can put my words on paper.
Who knows what I write, or the images my mind paints.
I can hear my breath,
like a sea, searching a shore.

II

Today I saw the skull again,
lousy with love the final flesh
had turned to worms.

The bones move with other life,
while the sky's throat cries another light.
And another circle swallows the tree.

I do not see it happen.
Somewhere, in the closed fist of possibility,
a handful of future moans.

Biography

All that has been written about women by men should be suspect, for the men are at once judge and party to the law suit. – Poulain de la Barre, 17th century feminist.

You have observed the rising
and the setting of my star,
calculated where you are in my orbit
with a mathematical accuracy
fine-tuned to your own needs.
Your forked tongue charms my constellations.
The tender yarn is drawn from my silkworm heart
and made to steel.

I am the other side of blood.
A screech of light that tries for breath.
No-one holds my beacon.
Women friends have gone
like dew on morning leaves,
their steps smooth as water on familiar stones,
soundless with desertion.

My letters and photographs
you prepare as a surgeon for an operation.
Your cacophony confounds my tune.
You sift my words and tear apart my truth.
The connective tissue jerks and kicks,
and fails.
It will not let you make it
the ache of your ribs.

ELIZABETH I

(a fifteen part poem)

Diary of 100,000 Devils

(i.m. Edith Sitwell)

'Your Lordship will see what a pretty business it is to have to deal with this woman who I think must have 100,000 devils . . .'
Bishop De Quadra, Spanish Ambassador.

I

The axe grows cold!
Throckmorton's horse comes fast
across the autumn leaves.
He brings her jewel.
I know already who will rule!

This is the Lord's doing . . . it is marvellous in our eyes.

Mother. Headless skeleton, slept 20 years,
forget your pains.
The 'little bastard' reigns!

I am mettlesome.
My hair is flames!
See. My eye is imperious –
They *will* bow low!
And they must watch my temper . . .
At the first blush of my cheek, silence!

My death rattle does not come until I will it.

Mother, now your story will begin again.

Mother, now your story will begin again.
I have escaped the axe.
Watch your little witch make England great!

II

See. My wrists are thin.
Women do not wield a sword well.
I recoil from death.

I *will* have peace.
Disastrous wars, extravagance,
are done with –
Come. Be merry! Dance! Write poetry!

My suitors I'll bewitch,
make magic like a fine tune on a lute.
This is how I shall do it –
I am in no hurry . . .

Spun from the pure wisdom of childhood,
my webs are intricate.
I shall wear my best gowns, diamonds, pearls.
My skin is milk white. See. It glows.
My eye pretends.

Everything depends on the husband she takes . . . says Feria.
He thinks he plays me like a game of chess.
They say I have one hundred thousand devils.
Good God! Give me strength!

This fervour, this religious fray chews up my bones.
My shoulder turns.
I watch the very air I breathe in case it burns.

III

Oh, Leicester, Leicester.
Master of The Horse.
He who sired your father, he who sired you,
have long gone to the block.
It screams out – *Vulture! Traitor!*
Be not censured.

Rumours circulate –
Your wife died, neck burst on the stair . . .
We two born same day, same hour, shall be as one.
My blood draws through your air,
my breath, your breath, heaven knows . . .
My love! My spirit! Take it, quick! It is my flesh!

IV

So she is tall, they say.
Too tall, I think.
For I am as a woman should be – perfect sized.

My waist is small.
My eyes slant, haunt.
And when I hold my head in this way . . .
that . . .
well . . .
I am all I need of height.

– What right has she to put my country on her Coat of Arms!

Stuart!
She moves in. Courageous. Beautiful.
Although they say she has a lack of scruple.
That ingredient may do the trick.
I'll think on it.

V

So now she has a son! Wise as Solomon?
Her skirts heave. This is hilarious!

I have sent her yet again my barbed regard.
The present of a font, baptismal, in enamelled gold.
She thinks I will be godmother to this child.
Is she mad? My blood runs cold.

My son keeps good company with higher hosts.
I will not have him in this Pandemonium. *Accursed death!*

The axe sparks on the nuptial ring.
Inside that band of gold a demon chortles,
draws its hold, tight. Kills.

VI

I pray! I pray! I pray!
Let them not say that I was cruel.
Let them not say I did not love.
I have done all I can with this religious mania.
Dear God? What have they done with you?
Blood! Blood! Blood!
I'm sick with it.

Must it be she who makes me do this –

Mary . . .

I who let the block rot, fall apart, must now
make new that gormandizing firth for Norfolk!
Ah, desp...ai...ai...r
When will it cease?

VII

Oh, dark secret!
You who wake me nightly with the quick sharp bite of love
from my bold dreams –
come, hold me, hold me.
Ugh! This sickness. This convulsing need. This loneliness.
The axe a thousand fold were better . . .

My ambassadors have sturdy feet, their eye is keen.
They know my cunning, take my messages as seas of leaves
for princes to wade in.
You, my England have my hand!
I tremble, grow bold with the elements.
My people! All my essences are yours –
My spring, my summer, autumn, winter.
Oh, be loyal, for my Royal blood seeks out your hearts.

VIII

This is fabulous!
This sugar, spice . . .
Drake has brought me Paradise!
Gold and silver, emeralds from Peru!
It is more than the income of the English Crown for an entire year.

He is a skilled navigator.
The Spaniards would like him on the gallows.
I shall knight him!
We will colonise remote and barbarous lands
where no prince ever laid a hand before!

IX

And now this cub . . .
Francois de Valois, tests his ore.
He is young, tender in opinion,
and he makes me laugh.

– More difficult to manage
than the rest –
But the fulcrum falters with this king of Spain –
Incarnate menace!

I will have my country first!

Francois de Valois, Duc de Alencon, *the frog*.
Tell me, in which pool does this one swim?
I'll pour elixirs into it, see how he drinks.

X

Over and over again I am finding loop-holes for this woman!
Will she never learn?
She fuels my enemies and sparks up fire.
Although . . . there is a thread of sisterhood flows through our
blood.

It is her head they want, my parliament.
They say she'll be my poison chalice . . .

Mary . . .

* * *

Someone told me she wore blood-red silk beneath her gown,
a martyr's robe.
She would.

It took the axe three blows to take her head.
And yet, she might have lived had there been something else
to knot us . . . though it drifts . . .

Mary, Queen of Scots, and I, Elizabeth.
Two girls who learned from shadows, walls, the mouths of gods,
the name of *PAIN* too soon.

XI

We are invincible!
The tongues of God are with us! See the fire!
Our modern guns and cannons, lighter ships,
perplex their ponderous galleons with their swarming oars
ablink like fast bewildered eyes.

Their sailors lie in the sea's depths with their cannon balls,
all passion spent.
And the young Prince of Ascolo, Phillip's son, they say,
floats on the waves,
legs russet silk, white satin breeches, like a dead fish in the sun.

Drake's mastery is plain. The Spanish will not dare our seas again!

XII

Summer 1588! Poets sing to *Gloriana*
make of me a goddess –
Though my hair is thin I have exquisite wigs.
And see my gems!
Love, sweet love, shines from my soul! I glow, your queen!

I hide beneath these tumbling silks, this lace, these emeralds.
You do not see my missing teeth, my wrinkled skin–

But one by one you leave me –
Walsingham, then Drake, then Burleigh.
But the worst –
and first to go.
Oh, Leicester! My dear heart.

I search your void. I seek your eye. I seek your laugh –
Eternity, how dark you are. Where do your tunnels go?
Oh, long, long, long, long Time.

XIII

Someone walks fast down these corridors.
Leicester's stepson, Essex, comes.
He warms my heart. He writes of love. He flatters.
Let it be.
These dying years are slow. He knows their tune.

I slap his arm. It is hard muscle.
His laughter is white teeth and tendons.

Nightly I hold my ageing body.
The skin grows loose, the flesh draws in.
Oh, Essex! Essex! cries a girl somewhere.
She did not live. Forgive.

XIV

Why does he pain me so?
Blunders. Losses.
Foolish bravura.
He is trying now to cause my people to rebel
against their queen.
He thinks me old, maternal tired,
calls my mind a carcase. This is treason!
Love twists back upon itself again and I am torn.
Elizabeth. Elizabeth. Breathe. Take his head!

XV

And so I moan, like a lonely dog out in the night.
Sweet England's Pride, is gone.
My body drains itself of tears.
I try to dance, give audience,
and wonder, in my small space now – where does a queen go,
when she's out of phase?

I have sold lands, jewels.
Today I wrote to Parliament again: A new subsidy.
My ladies-in-waiting talk:
She is forgetful – weary – longs for lost loves – fears ghosts.

My feet sound light upon the corridors.
My gowns trail on my failing frame.
And once I saw my body, thin and fearful in a flame.

I took my leave of Parliament this week.
The words choked in my throat.
I said I did not plan to reign, longer than was good for them,
and though I wasn't wise or mighty,
maybe I had loved them more, than any monarch had before.

And now . . . I contemplate my mother.
Dare to think of that sad ghost.
The chill of death comes close.
I do not eat. I do not sleep.
Who is it comes now to my door?
I hear my mother, weep.

ACKNOWLEDGEMENTS

Some of these poems have appeared in *Acumen, Yes, I Like This Poem* (edited by Christopher North), *Poet's England: Cheshire* (edited by Gladys Mary Coles), and *Poet's England: Derbyshire* (edited by Alison Chisholm). Others have been heard on BBC Radio Network North West's *Write Now*. Thanks are due to the editors of these, and to Gladys Mary Coles for making this collection possible.

WENDY BARDSLEY is also a non-fiction writer with Longman Books and works as a freelance lecturer for University Departments of Professional Development. While working in the Greater Manchester Education Inspection and Advisory Service she was responsible for matters concerning the United Nations Convention of the Rights of the Child.

She lives in Marple, Cheshire, and is actively involved with poetry in the Greater Manchester area